Acclaim for *l*

MW00678536

"As ever, Bil Lepp turns the mundane into the sublime—and in *Muddling Through* thoughtfully and powerfully translates adult and kid perspectives on parenting moments. Who better than a master storyteller with a choice yarn to connect parents and children on the things that really matter."

—William Weil, Co-Founder and CEO, Tales2Go

"When you finish this book, you'll probably start wishing that the Lepp family would adopt you. Or if that's too drastic, then you'll at least want to come back in another life as their family dog. OR, maybe you'll just start small, and ask them to take you on a road trip. I could totally be trapped in a car for a week with these people."

"Finally a parenting book that reminds us that if you and your family can laugh through this crazy pressure cooker of life….you're probably doing it right."

—Mindy Thomas, Host of The Absolutely Mindy Show on Sirius XM's Kids Place Live

MUDDLING THROUGH

PERSPECTIVES ON
PARENTING

MUDDLING THROUGH

PERSPECTIVES ON

PARENTING

BIL LEPP

**AWARD-WINNING
STORYTELLER**

Copyright © 2012 by Bil Lepp

All rights reserved.

Published by Familius LLC, www.familius.com

Familius books are available at special discounts for bulk purchases for sales promotions, family or corporate use. Special editions, including personalized covers, excerpts of existing books, or books with corporate logos, can be created in large quantities for special needs. For more information, contact Premium Sales at 801-552-7298 or email specialmarkets@familius.com

Library of Congress Catalog-in-Publication Data
LCCN: 2012945114
eISBN: 978-1-938301-02-5
pISBN: 978-1-938301-03-2

Printed in the United States of America

Book design by Marissa Empey
Illustrations by Bil Lepp
Jacket design by David Miles
Edited by Edith Songer

10 9 8 7 6 5 4 3 2 1

First Edition

 HELPING FAMILIES BE HAPPY

To Ellie and Noah, my prime subjects,
& Paula, my chief co-muddler.

*   *   *

Introduction

When I was asked to write this book it was not because I am an accredited child rearing expert. I have no degree, credential, or recognition as a child raising expert. I am a professional storyteller who occasionally tells stories about parenting. Here's an important credential I do hold: I have won the West Virginia Liars' Contest five times. I am a fiction writer and a humorist. As a champion liar and a fiction writing humorist, I sometimes make stuff up. So, the funny little stories that begin each chapter of this book didn't necessarily happen exactly the way I present them. They happened, more or less, but I have taken the liberty of occasionally crafting some events in the vignettes to better illustrate the points I am trying to make.

The advice I offer, however, is honest. I have two kids who, at this writing, are eight and eleven years old. That gives me nineteen collective years in the parenting trenches. I cannot claim to be a successful parent. I'm not sure when any parent can deem their job a success. Your child's whole life will be greatly determined by the portion they spend with you. I am offering what advice I can with the idea that I think my wife and I are doing pretty well. I hope our experiences help you.

Finally, in the interest of full disclosure, I should admit that I have never before written an advice book, never read an advice book, and don't have much intention of ever reading one. I'm not sure I've ever even read an instruction manual past the point where it says, "Before attempting to operate this device you need to thoroughly read these instructions." I just muddle through.

Best Regards,

Bil Lepp

Eiger Mountain, Switzerland (not really... I just like Clint Eastwood movies, and authors always end their forewords by stating some exotic location. Actually, I'm on the couch in the living room.)

Table of Contents

CHAPTER 1

About Conversations and Questions

Daddy Dog Killer

I know that children tend to ask a lot of questions, but there are times when I think my kids have been secretly attending Congressional panels to hone their interrogation techniques. My kids are young, eleven and eight years old, so you'd think I'd notice if they slipped off to Washington for week or so. I'm not that inattentive a parent. I don't know—maybe they're upstairs watching C-Span right now.

Driving along in the minivan, when I'm pretty sure the kids are asleep in the backseat, I'll risk saying something innocent to my wife such as, "Did you see that dog crossing the road back there?"

And then from the backseat I hear a noise that sounds suspiciously like a gavel falling, and my daughter says something like, "The Chairwoman recognizes the boy from the left side of the car."

My son clears his throat and intones, "Did you say a dog was on the road?"

And before I can answer, my daughter asks, "What color was the dog?"

There is an intensity to the questions. For the next few minutes all that matters is that dog.

"Was the dog crossing the street from left to right? Or right to left?"

"Was it a big dog? Or a small dog?"

"Do you think the dog was rabid?"

"Was it a wild dog?"

"Was it a dingo?"

"Could it have been a kangaroo?"

I start to sweat under the scrutiny. I still haven't had a chance to answer even one of these questions. I'm looking for an opening. I reach out and grip my wife's hand. Why don't they ask her these questions? She saw the dog, too. "Brown. Brown!" I confess. "The dog was brown!"

"I see," comes the voice of my daughter. "Brown. Light brown or dark brown?"

Now my son jumps in, trying to confuse me. "What's the difference between a shade and a hue?" That's why you should never home school. Who taught my kid about hues? Not me. He probably learned it from one of those other home school kids during his astrophysics lab. Vocabulary thugs.

They're trying to break me down. But I'm sticking with my story. "Uh, light brown." I look at my wife for confirmation. She shrugs as if to say, "I never said I saw the dog." She drops my hand. She's distancing herself from me.

One of the kids spills their apple juice in the back seat. This is their variation of waterboarding.

"Was the dog all brown, or was he spotted?"

Why does any of this matter? I didn't really get a good look at the dog. I wish I'd never seen that dog! Stupid dog! "Mostly light brown, with some dark brown around the edges."

"Was the dog going left to right? Or right to left?"

Now we're back to this. "Right to left," I state confidently.

"Why was the dog crossing the road?" my daughter asks.

"To get to the other side," I try. Yeah. She didn't laugh either.

"Did you hit the dog?"

"No," I nearly cry.

"So the brown dog was crossing the road right to left, but you didn't hit it?"

"That's correct."

"And you have no reason to believe it was sick? You don't think it was rabid?"

"No."

"Was it foaming at the mouth?"

"No."

"If it had been rabid, would you have hit it?"

"I, I, I . . ."

"Have you ever hit a dog?"

"Do you know anyone who has hit a dog?"

"Why do they call it the 'dog days of summer'?"

"Who invented the hotdog?"

"What does 'dog tired' mean to you?"

"When can we get another dog?"

"What's a bounty hunter?"

"Would you have swerved into the other lane to hit the rabid dog?"

"I, I, I . . ."

My daughter asks, "What if there was a baby lying on the side of the road and the rabid dog was crossing the road to bite the baby? Then the baby would get rabies. Would you hit the dog then?"

"Yeah, Dad. Would you have swerved into the other lane to hit the rabid dog, even if there was a truck coming at you, to save a baby?"

My daughter sighs, "That poor rabies baby."

"Yes," I stammer, "I would hit the dog to save the baby."

My wife asks: "You'd risk all of our lives to swerve into the other lane in front of an oncoming truck? What if the baby was just a doll?"

Traitor.

I hate that dog. I know it is not nice, but I'd swerve across three lanes of traffic to hit that dog right now, rabid or not!

"Yeah, Dad. What if the baby was just a doll and the dog wasn't rabid, and the baby doll was the dog's toy, and he was crossing the road because he dropped his toy? You'd kill a dog for that?"

"Wait . . ." I protest. "I never said . . ."

"Was the dog mostly light brown with just a little bit of dark brown?"

"Yes, yes. Just like that."

My daughter giggles. "Just like a Reese's cup."

"Yes," I agree, "sort of like a Reese's."

"Can we stop and get a Reese's cup?" the kids ask in unison.

What can the dog killer do? I pull into a Go-Mart and we adjourn for a Reese's break. It may be my only chance to rid myself of the dog.

*   *   *

YOUR children are most likely not asking you questions for the sole purpose of annoying you. It may seem that way, but I doubt they are asking just for that reason.

Everybody needs to talk to their children. And you need to talk to your children about things your kids want to talk about. This means answering myriad and seemingly endless strands of questions. This is how kids learn. It is also how parents learn.

Adults

A lot of times kids will ask you questions to which you don't know the answer, which will lead into a question to which you also don't know the answer. This is annoying for several reasons. The first reason is because you feel like an idiot. You are driving down the road, in the driver's seat, in command as it were, and you are thinking to yourself, "I'm an idiot. How have I gotten to this stage in life without knowing the basic difference between a fruit and a vegetable?" Don't feel bad. Having children is a daily exercise in finding out what you don't know. Just be honest.

Kids

Don't get frustrated with your parents, either. They know a lot, but sometimes you need to help them remember that they know more than they think they know. Your job, children, is to ask, ask, ask. The thing is, sometimes adults misunderstand your questions. We think we are answering your questions, but you are looking for something more. Sometimes you need to ask your question a different way. For example, my son once asked, "Dad, which way do the planets go around the Sun?"

"In a circle," I said. (I later learned, from my son, that the planets don't travel in a circle, but an ellipse.)

He huffed. This was not the answer he was looking for. "I know that, but what direction?"

I pursed my lips. I had no idea. "I'm not sure. I'm not sure if they go clockwise or counter clockwise."

Another huff. My son was getting frustrated with

my answers, but he hung in there, certain he could pry the information out of my head if he just kept coming at it from different angles. "Okay," he said, "what I mean is, do the planets go around the Sun like a merry-go-round or like a Ferris wheel?"

My response was a definite and profound, "Drrrrr? I uh…I have never in all my years though about it. When I was in school all the models of the solar system had the planets going around the Sun like a merry-go-round."

"Why?" he asked.

I didn't know that answer either, but I offered what I knew: "The thing about space is that "Up" and "Down" are concepts that we apply on Earth because we have a ground and a sky. In space, there isn't really an up or a down. There is just space. So I guess the direction the planets go around the Sun would depend on the direction from which you were looking at them." I gave myself a mental high-five. I felt pretty good about that answer.

I had not answered the boy's question. I didn't know the answer to his original question, but because we both stuck with the conversation, we eventually came to a point where we were both satisfied. He got the best answer I could give; I gave the best answer I could give.

Another reason the questions are annoying is because you are trying to listen to NPR or ESPN or Fox News while you are driving home from swim practice. Here's the thing—when you decided to have a kid, you agreed to an unwritten but important contract in which you acknowledged that your child was going to be more important than Scott Van Pelt or Click & Clack. (However, if you are lucky the kids will eventually come to enjoy *Car Talk*.) Having a child means giving more of yourself and more of your time than you might have first imagined, but if you are going to be a good parent you need to fight the urge to shush and muzzle the kids.

One of the most important lessons I have learned through my kids is that I know more than I thought I did. If you let the questions go on long enough, your kid is eventually going to ask a question to which you know the answer. From the back of the car comes the question, "Dad, how many men are in a regiment?"

"Uh, I'm not sure."

"How many regiments are in an Army?"

"Don't know."

"Does a squadron of planes have as many planes as

a squad of infantry has soldiers?

"Couldn't say."

"How many countries fought in World War Two?"

"Most of the countries in the world were committed to the war effort in one way or another."

"Which countries fought with the Axis?"

And just like that, you know the answer to something.

No matter how many questions you can't answer, no matter how many times you say, "I don't know," your kids still believe you know everything. They have unfailing faith in your knowledge. If you get frustrated or angry at them for asking questions you are going to teach them that acquiring knowledge can be dangerous.

Sometimes you can circumvent the holes in your knowledge by answering questions with questions. If your kid asks, "What is the difference between a fruit and a vegetable?" you can ask, "Why do you want to know?"

With any luck, your child will say, "Because I was wondering if a tomato is a fruit or a vegetable."

Perhaps you know the answer to that question. (A tomato is a fruit.)

CHAPTER 2

About Having Fun

Cookie Cutters

LAST Christmas I told the kids to head to the kitchen. It was time to make sugar cookies. I like to make sugar cookies because they are easy and delicious. You mix the ingredients, put them in the fridge for a few hours, roll them out, cut them into shapes, and decorate them.

I have very few rules for the sugar cookie making process. No matter the season, I get out all the cookie cutters. My goal in making the sugar cookies is to have fun and let the kids express their creativity. If they want to make a green and red jack-o'-lantern at Christmas, that's fine by me. Mutant Ninja Star of David? I love it. Vampire Santa? Let it roll. Again, my object here is to have fun.

And to get cookies.

When we make cookies I keep in mind that we are
not making these cookies to give to the Wise Men to
give to Jesus. We are not making them for the queen
or the president. We are making them to have fun,
so it does not matter how they turn out.

There is enough work involved in making sugar
cookies that everyone has something to do, but
sugar cookies are simple enough that no one person
has too much to do—unless that one person is stuck
cleaning up the mess.

Speaking of mess, making cookies is sometimes a
thing we do when Mom is otherwise engaged. It
isn't that we don't want Mom to help make cookies,
it is just that it's easier to manage the mess without
Mom's help.

This past Christmas my kids and I whipped up,
chilled, and rolled out the dough (that could be a
hip-hop song) same as ever. By the way, rolling
out the dough is the hardest part of the whole
process. I suggest you lay some parchment paper
on the table and spread a bit of flour before you
start to roll. If worse comes to worst and you can't
get the cut dough off the table, you can just lift the
parchment paper onto the cookie sheet and cook
the cookies on the paper. Keep all water away

from the rolling pin. A little water on the rolling pin means sticky, sticky dough.

We had, of course, quite an array of cookie cutters. My daughter was focusing on Santa shapes and Christmas trees. My daughter likes to bake more than my son does. This is not a sexist comment or a political stance; it is just a fact. My son is older and I introduced him to making cookies before my daughter was ever born, but he hasn't taken to it like she has. My daughter has an artistic flair and she greatly enjoys the decorating process. She will spend hours carefully administering colored sugar so that her Santas end up wearing tartan sweaters, argyle socks, and plaid toy bags. She will separate the colored sprinkles to make sure her Christmas trees are top of the line.

My son was cutting out dozens of little stars and arranging them in a careful pattern on the cookie sheet.

"What's that?" I asked.

"Orion, Taurus, and the Pleiades," he said.

Duh.

This past year I decided to introduce icing into the whole process. I bought a tub of standard white

15

icing. We stirred some sugar into the icing so that it glittered like real ice on the edges of our trees and on our snowmen.

My daughter asked, "Can we add food coloring to this?"

Here is another reason it is sometimes best to make cookies when Mom is otherwise occupied: Kids and dads sometimes have good ideas which moms might frown on if they are forewarned. As soon as my daughter asked about food coloring, all three of us began to chuckle.

When Mom came to see how we were doing she was greeted by an army of glittering, icing smothered, yellow snowmen.

Delicious.

*　　　*　　　*

THE thing about fun is that it is supposed to be fun. One reason I like making cookies is because there are no serious consequences if the process goes wrong or the cookies don't turn out just right. We are not baking cookies to win a prize; we are baking cookies to spend time together. This is an important aspect to keep in mind when you are having fun. This is why I get out all the cookie cutters and let the kids make what they want to make. If they want to make a shape for which we have no cutter, I give them a knife. It is never too early to introduce cutlery into your child's play time. Well, maybe that's not completely true, but you know what I mean. I want them to have the power to express their creative sides and their senses of humor. That's what the cookie process is all about.

The cookie baking process is also about teaching the kids about the kitchen, but I don't mention that to them. I am not a chef, but I can cook the basics. A good way to learn your way around the kitchen is do something like baking cookies. It is an entertaining way to learn. You could take your kids on a tour of the kitchen, "Here's the stove. This is how you turn it on. This is a cookie sheet. This is flour…" but that is boring and probably won't stick. If you are cooking in the kitchen, then your kids are learning at least some survival skills. Imagine yourself saying to the kids, "You never know when you might end up stranded, alone, on a desert island with a full kitchen and a stocked pantry. You best know something about cooking so you don't starve."

Adults

If you are a parent then you have likely been angry with your children at some point in your parenting career. Having fun is about not getting angry. We often get all wrapped up in the right and wrong way to do things and thus we forget the fun way. We get all goal oriented. You don't always need to be goal oriented when you are having fun. Let the goal to which you are oriented be having fun. Drop the whole concept of 'good cookies' or 'correctly decorated cookies' and let loose. Take a deep breath and just adjust. Drop the dough? Make some more (or just scrape off the part that hit the floor). Burn the cookies? Oh well. Get food coloring on your clothes? You shouldn't be wearing your good clothes to begin with.

Kids

Your adults can get all uptight about the way things ought to be done. "Snowmen need to be white," they will tell you, "Trees need to have brown bark; pumpkins are orange." Bleck. You know, as kids, that the world can be any color you care to paint it. Tell your adults to ease up a bit. Challenge them to a contest. Tell them you want to see who can make the absolutely ugliest cookie. Tell them you want to make a story out of the cookies. Try getting them to help you make a scene from "Little Red Riding Hood." Make the best ever Red Riding Hood cookie decked out in red sugar and cinnamon hearts. Then, proclaim yourself the wolf and eat Red. If your brother eats your dough or breaks your turkey?

Don't strike back, just laugh it off and make another.

Kids and adults have very different views of the world. Adults have been worn down by the burden of being several decades old. The worst thing that happens to adults is that we acquire logic and skepticism along the way. We forget that as a child all things are possible. Adults have these weird concepts of "the odds," and "enough." Kids look at the world and see "chances," and "some."

If you say to an adult, "I'm going to enter this contest and win a free trip to Egypt," your adult will say, "Pfff, good luck. I bet a billion kids are entering that contest. Do you know the odds of you winning?"

As a kid, you do know your odds. They are pretty good. You are a good kid. You have a good chance of winning. That's the way the world should be.

Recently I looked out the window and about eleven tiny snowflakes were falling from the sky. "Hey kids, it's snowing," I said.

My kids jumped for joy like it was the blizzard of '78. "Let's go sledding!" they yelled.

When I pointed out the snow to the kids I wasn't saying, "Look, winter fun is on the way." I was saying, "Children, the climatic conditions associated with winter have in fact created a small amount of the traditional wintertime frozen precipitation."

It doesn't matter what I meant. The kids saw snow and they were ready to go sledding. My argument of "There isn't enough snow to go sledding," fell on deaf ears because to a kid any snow is enough snow to go sledding. Again, kids don't think about "enough." Kids think about "some." Some is enough to a kid—especially if you are talking about peas or broccoli.

As the adult you know sledding might be futile, but that is because you are thinking like an adult. Adults think in quantitative terms. The snow has to be so deep, the air so cold, the slope so steep... Think back to when you were a kid. Did you ever consider such things? As a child you did not go sledding, or biking, or swimming, or cookie baking with a specific set of requirements in mind for what would constitute quality fun. You just went and played.

Let it go, you knuckled-headed grown-up. Don't bring your expectations to the fun. Honestly, adult person, the amount of fun you have isn't quite as important as the amount of fun the child people with you have. Instead of making the kids play like you want them to, do as they do and play as they play. It'll make your day better.

Finally, you, as the adult, know that sledding means about an hour of you gathering the winter gear, pulling on coats, shoving on boots, zipping zippers, and tying laces so that you can go outside for fifteen minutes, slide down the hill twice, watch everybody get covered in mud, and then do the laundry.

Don't forget you still have to wash the dishes from the cookie baking, clean the table, sweep the floor, and put all the decorations away.

But look at those smiles.

CHAPTER 3

Wants and Needs
and the Value of Things

Don't Get Too Attached to Balloons

"**D**ON'T get too attached to those balloons," I pleaded with the kids. "One thing you can be sure of in this life is that the balloons won't be with us all that long."

My son was eight. He'd found a clown at a street fair who was twisting balloons into poodles and giraffes. Never one to settle for the simple, my son asked the clown for an octopus. I could see by the clown's expression that he was thinking, "Great. An eight legged sea creature. Just what I wanted to make out of balloons while balancing on eight-foot stilts. I should have gone into bookkeeping." That clown was a trouper though. He smiled, blew up four balloons, and started twisting away. Soon, there was a creature that had a big head and six legs. The clown handed it to my son. My son said, "It's only got six legs."

"Well," said the clown, "it's a six-topus."

My daughter was four. She just wanted a poodle. It's not every day a kid can make a clown happy.

While walking back to the car the six-topus suffered a heinous accident to one leg. "Well," I said. "Now you have a pentopus." Parenting is all about looking for the bright side. Parenting is also all about looking through the dictionary so you can make up words like pentopus.

My daughter's poodle exploded for no discernible reason. That left my daughter with nothing but the shattered and torn remnants of a white balloon and a little clown spit in her hand. "Well," I did not say, "now you have a corpse." Parenting is all about not going over to the dark side. Instead, I said, "It pays not to get too attached to balloons."

One weekend we hit the road for a three day trip. I'm a professional storyteller and tour often. When they can, my wife and kids join me. At one show a friendly old lady gave my daughter a handful of helium balloons. As we were getting into the van one of the balloons escaped. I watched the balloon head toward the clouds, and then I looked back at my daughter. Her face was locked into that silent, bitter, heartbreaking sob that only four-year-olds can manufacture. I thought she'd been stung by a wasp. Or bitten by a snake. Or that she had just seen her mother carried off by rabid camels. "What's wrong?" I asked.

She gasped, pointed at the balloon disappearing into the sky, and managed to say, "Oh, Daddy, that… that… that was your favorite balloon!"

Up to that point I hadn't realized that I had a favorite balloon. I thought I hated all balloons equally. I try not to get too attached to balloons. I thought fast. "No. No," I said, "this is my favorite balloon." I snatched a balloon from her remaining handful. "See?" I explained. "Mine has a white ribbon." I pointed at the balloon now barely visible above the distant tree line. "That one has a blue ribbon."

"Are you sure?" my daughter asked doubtfully.

"Sure I'm sure." Parenting is all about lying.

I've heard it said that if you have kids you should have a pet, one reason being that the pet will eventually die and then you can explain about loss and death to your kids. I'm not sure that that is the best reason to have a pet—certainly the pet might have something to say on the subject. We did have a great dog for years, and then he got sick and passed on. I guess it was good for the kids to learn that lesson. We didn't get the dog just so he would die, but after many years he finally, and inevitably, did. We were attached to the dog.

The poor dog had a tumor on his head and it was obvious that he was ill. The obvious tumor didn't do a thing for the dog, but it did make the dog's plight easier to understand for the children. They could see that he was ill and thus it was easier to explain to the kids what was happening. When the dog, Buck-dog, eventually passed, the kids were ready for it. No one was happy about it, but everyone was prepared.

Balloons, on the other hand, are not as handy for teaching kids about loss and death. The main reason being that a balloon will be sitting there perfectly calm on the kitchen floor and then explode for no apparent reason at all. One second the balloon is there making us all happy; the next moment it is a choking hazard. This sort of violent demise seldom happens to domestic pets.

You can envision eventually saying to your kids, "Well, Granny got sick and died just like Buck-

25

dog." I seriously doubt that I will ever have to say, "Well kids, Granny just all of the sudden popped. One second she was sitting there, and the next…" I'm not saying it won't happen; I'm just saying I doubt it will happen. So, I advise my kids not to get too attached to balloons.

*   *   *

LITTLE kids attach extreme importance to things adults think insignificant. What's more, kids attach this value quickly and without obvious discretion. A stone, a penny, a balloon, an action figure, a stuffed animal, or blanket can instantaneously become the most important thing in the world. There will be no road trip, no bedtime, no going to Grandma's until said object is found and secured.

Adults

It is important for children to value and take responsibility for their possessions. It is important for adults to teach kids which things are essential and which things can be lived without for the time being. Sometimes this can be done by helping the child understand what you are trying accomplish. "We are trying to go see a movie, young Suzi. You want to go see the movie, right? The movie starts in twenty minutes. If we don't go now, we won't be able to go at all. Can we look for your old, used, dirty, chewed-up but intrinsically valuable popsicle stick when we get home?" In many cases you can get your child to prioritize if they see the bigger picture. They might not be happy about it, but they'll soon recover. Furthermore, kids forget quickly. There is a good chance little Suzi will have completely forgotten about the popsicle stick three minutes later.

Kids

Sometimes your adults just don't get why things are important to you. Sometimes you have to explain it to them. There are times when you need to say, "That is not just a chewed up popsicle stick. That stick is from the popsicle Grandpa gave me when we visited his house last time." Look around, kids. We adults have a ton of stuff. TVs, stoves, cars, stuff on the shelves, stuff in the closet, stuff on the floor. All of it means something to us. Do you remember a time when your mom or dad couldn't find their keys or their wallet or cell phone or iPod? What did they do? They ran around the house throwing a fit, didn't they? "Where's my wallet? Who took my wallet?" If you think about it, they were acting just like you act when you lose something important. A wallet or a phone is an important thing that often has great value to your adult. But does that wallet have more value to your adult than your stuffed bear has to you? Nope. So, you may need to remind

your adults, in a calm way, that what you own is just
as important to you as what they own is to them.

Children screaming in a supermarket about an item
THEY MUST HAVE can cause quite a ruckus, but
giving in only causes problems. Say "No" and press
on with your shopping. Children need to know that
not every want is a need. They need to learn thrift.
Most importantly, they need to know that you have
a stronger will than they. A three-year-old that gets
everything they want every time they throw a fit is
going to be one intolerable teenager.

One thing you need to get into your head as a
parent is that you are raising your child to the best
of your abilities. Set your standards, and don't fret
too much about what others think of your parenting
style. If people in Target see me denying my child a
toy she wants, and they think I am mean, oh well. I
know what I'm trying to teach my kid, and I don't
care much what you think of me. I look at a sad,
screaming child throwing a fit in the supermarket
and just smile when the parent with them simply
ignores the tantrum. That parent is raising a
responsible child.

Adults

I look at it like this—stores are set up to make
people want to buy things. You take a kid into a

store and you are asking for a tantrum. The thing is, they throw the tantrum because they have a physical force—you—blocking the way to what they want. What about you? How hypocritical are you when you go into a store? What are you teaching your kids if you to say them, "We're just going in to get a gallon of milk, three carriage bolts, and a ceiling fan." And then along the way you decide you need a Maglite, a soda, some doughnuts, and a hairbrush. The only difference between your and your child's buy-impulse in that situation is that there is no one telling you, "You can't buy that flashlight." What if there was? What if you had to take an authority figure into the store who said, "Nope, you can't have that."

You would throw a fit. Keep that in mind. You need to model the kind of person you want your child to be.

Everyone has an idea and opinion on how you should raise your child. You and your spouse, partner, co-parent, or you alone if you're a single parent, need to decide on your approach and stick to it. That's not to say you shouldn't be open to advice (I mean, here you are reading a book full of advice), but you need to stick to your guns. I've had to tell my own mother that while I appreciated her advice, I was also going to ignore it. I live with my kids every day and I know the methods I am employing.

Our son was born premature and the muscles
he needed to suckle weren't developed. He had
a hard time eating. He was born at just over five
pounds and stayed tiny for a long time. People
constantly told my wife, "You need to feed that
baby," as if she hadn't thought of that herself.
There were two guys at church we called Biscuit
and Gravy because each Sunday that is what
they said we should be feeding our newborn.
We understood our son's condition. We were in
communication with the doctor. We knew what we
were doing. A woman at a store said to my wife,
"Your child looks sickly. You should feed him
more." At the end of her rope, my generally sweet
wife replied, "I think he's doing pretty well for a
child born without an esophagus." It wasn't the
kindest thing my wife could have said, but it was
doggone funny.

So, be it your child or an unsolicited counselor, stick
to your guns. Momma knows best.

Start teaching your children from day one what is a
need and what is a want. Then help them attach the
proper value to things. In other words, don't get too
attached to balloons. Balloons were never meant to
be keepsakes. We need to tell our kids what things
they can expect to stay around forever and what
things are fleeting. This helps them develop realistic
expectations.

I knew a kid who knew what a dollar was, and
what you could do with a dollar, but he had no
concept of saving. He would do most anything to
get a dollar. "Hey kid, I'll give a dollar if you get
me the remote." Hey kid, "I'll give you a buck if
you go get me a glass of water." This might seem
an excessive and expensive way to get things done,
but here's the thing: you would give the kid a dollar
and he would be joyous. For about sixty seconds.
Then he would get diverted from the dollar and he
would lay it down. At that point, you could pick
the dollar up and give the same dollar back to the
kid five minutes later for yet another task. You
could pay that little guy the same dollar a hundred
times a day. It was a neat little trick, until he finally
developed the concept of saving. Then you couldn't
get him to do anything for a dollar.

Kids have short memories and they rebound
quickly. A child throwing an "I must have it or I
will die!" fit in the cereal aisle is generally happy as
a lark by the time you get to the car.

Kids

If you really want something, think about it before
you leave for the store. If you think you might
want something, ask your folks if you can take
five dollars out of your bank to take with you to
the store. If you have your own money you have a

31

better argument for getting what you want.

Adults

Ask yourself, "What is the value my kid is placing on this lost item?" Why is it important to her?" Also, remember that if you put a toy catalogue in front of a kid and say, "Go through there and circle the things you want for your birthday," that kid is going to circle everything in the book and then wonder why, after you offered the world, you are not providing it. It never hurts to limit the choices.

Finally, diffuse the situation. I try and turn things into games. One game I like is "How Many?" My kid will say, "Oh, Daddy, I want that doll baby." And I'll say, "How many do you want?" This throws the kid. They were waiting for a "Yes" or "No." I just changed the equation. My kid will consider and say, "I want a hundred of those dolls." I say, "And what would you do with all of them?"

By that time, we are past the dolls and having a conversation. Furthermore, you kid has your attention, which is most likely all they wanted in the first place.

CHAPTER 4

About Traditions

Bending Candles

WHEN I was a kid my family always went to
church on Christmas Eve out of reverence to
the season. When I was a teenager we went for
reverence but also because my dad had become a
pastor. We go now with my family because it seems
the right thing to do with the kids on Christmas
Eve. The two things that mean the most to me
in any Christmas Eve service are singing "Silent
Night" and the little candle each person receives as
they enter the service. Every Christmas Eve service
I have ever attended, no matter the location or the
denomination, I have received a white, four- or
five-inch candle with a little paper disk to keep
melted wax from dripping on your hand. The

candles are handed out so that the parishioners can light them, one person passing the light to the next in a symbolic act of spreading the word of Christ into the world, as we all sing "Silent Night." And that little candle is an integral part of my whole Christmas experience.

I don't know when it started, but I know why it started. That candle was, and always has been, my central diversion during the long, dark, Christmas Eve service. When I was a kid I needed something to do in the sanctuary to ease my boredom during church services. During regular church services I would draw on the bulletins, but I couldn't draw during the Christmas Eve service because it was always dark. Thus the candle became my refuge— but not in some metaphorical "light the candle against the darkness" kind of way, or even in some theological "Jesus is the light of the world" sense.

As soon as I was nestled safely in the pew I would strip the paper shield off the candle and then grasp the candle as tight as I could in my hand. Throughout the service, through all the hymns, through all the prayers, through all the up and downs, through the long, slow drudgery of the sermon, I would hold that candle in the tightest grip I could muster.

The goal of the activity was to warm the wax of

the candle so much with my body heat that I could
bend the candle, mold it, twist it, reshape it into
some glorious new form. But each year, it seemed,
I gave in too soon. "Try it now," a little voice
would call in my head. "Try it now. It's been long
enough." And so fifteen minutes into the service I
would try and bend the candle, and sixteen minutes
into the service I would have a broken candle. Then
I would squeeze the two halves in my hand trying
to create enough heat to melt them back together.
By the time we got around to singing "Silent Night"
my candle would be a series of wax chunks held
tenuously together by the wick, looking far more
like a cheap, broken, fake pearl necklace than a
candle. And then I would have to wait anxiously a
whole 'nother year to try it again. Oh, the agony!
Each year trying to stifle the voice and hold out one
more minute—one more minute.

I know that somewhere in every church there is a
box of white candles, some broken, sitting on the
shelf of a storeroom. I know that I could go into
any church, any day of the year, grab a handful of
candles, and sit in my living room, watching TV and
squeezing candles until they are soft enough to bend.
But this act of reshaping the candles has no meaning,
and no place, outside of the Christmas Eve service.
It is an act of transformation that has meaning only
within the structure of the Christmas Eve service.
Outside of the service there would simply be no

reason to squeeze a candle until I could bend it. It might even seem silly outside of the Christmas Eve service. Eight thousand, seven hundred and fifty-nine hours out of the year I can look at little white candles and never think twice about subjecting them to the tortures and ministrations of holding and twisting them into new forms, but as soon as I start to get dressed for the Christmas Eve service, my anticipation starts to grow.

And now I have children. In whispered conversations, so their mother doesn't hear, I say, "You only get one candle, you only get one chance a year. It's not about success, it's about the act itself."

"What are you three talking about?" my wife asks.

"Nothing," I lie. "A Christmas surprise."

And then back to the children, "The goal, for me, is to make a circle out of the candle, but I've never achieved that goal. So, the real goal is to keep on trying to accomplish the goal."

"Are you talking about bending candles?" my wife asks.

"Nope," the three of us all say very unsuspiciously.

"We're not going to the Christmas Eve service to play

with candles," she explains to the children. And me. "We're going to celebrate the birth of Jesus."

She grew up Baptist; she's been conditioned to believe church is just about God and Jesus.

I wink at the kids.

With barely concealed desire I reach for my candle when we arrive at the church. I lick my lips as the kid manning the box hands over a candle. I try not to snatch it. The kids get theirs. I examine mine to make sure there are no cracks or faults. It must be perfect. I grip it in my hand even before we are settled. The kids have theirs held tightly, too. I can feel my body heat transferring to the cold wax.

I have an advantage over the kids because I'm an adult, thus my hand is bigger. I can heat up a larger section of the candle. And, I've been doing this for nearly forty years. I have the patience that comes from experience. Fifteen minutes into the service the voice starts, "Try it now. Try it now." "No," I shout silently back at the voice. "Not this year! This the year I hold out!"

But something strange is happening in the service. The lights are off, as usual, and the greens are hung, and the acolytes have lit other candles all around the church, but something is wrong. There's a tension in the church. And then I see it. One set of greens, actual boughs from a pine tree, real pine needles that have been hanging in the church for a month, drying out in the heat, are way too close to one of the big Christmas candles. Everybody sees it, but nobody is going to do a thing about it. It's too good a diversion. Everybody is asking themselves the same question, "Will the candle burn down fast enough, or will it set the church on fire?"

By the time we get to the sermon, it's pretty clear the greens aren't going to catch fire. The mood of the congregation has gone flat. Deflated. My children are each trying to melt the broken halves of their candles back together. I've managed to hold out. "A few more minutes," I tell myself. "You're an adult. You can hold out a little longer."

Now, this particular church's sound system has an odd quirk. For reasons beyond my ken, the system will sometimes, and quite randomly, pick up bits of conversations being broadcast by truckers on their CBs as they pass by the church on the nearby highway. And the truckers do not always use church sanctioned language.

So as the preacher intoned, "On this most holy of nights, when Joseph and Mary made their way by donkey…"

And then a trucker broke in, "Big Billy? D'you see that Mustang go by?"

"Ten-four, Outlaw Pete. I saw it. That dude was really flying, and there was a hot lil' mamma in the passenger seat."

Celestial commentary.

The preacher, a bit befuddled, paused to make sure the truckers were done. "The three wise men saw a star in the East…"

"Big Billy? Outlaw Pete? This is Hamhock. I see a Smokey's lights up ahead. I think your Mustang mighta got pulled over."

Even the preacher chuckled at that. He told the sound man to switch off the PA system before we heard anymore.

The best part about it was that it had kept my mind off the candle in my hand. The service was winding down. I'd almost made it. My children watched with awe as I began to slowly, ever so slowly, bend my candle. It was going to happen! I was going to— snap. I sighed out loud. Loud enough that people would have looked at me, except that at that very moment, the candle under the dried pine branch hanging in the window rallied, sending out a long

39

lick of flame that lit the greens above the window. It was as though the candle in the window had waited until everyone had forgotten about it—moved on to other things—before it lit the greens. There was a mad flurry of activity as people rushed to put the fire out.

I was concentrated on the candle in my hand. I'd bent it so far that there was no way I was going to be able to repair it unless I could somehow straighten it out. Snap. The kids chuckled.

The pastor got the congregation back in the pews. The smell of burned pine filled the room. There was smoke hanging near the ceiling. But we hadn't sung "Silent Night." And it ain't Christmas 'til you sing "Silent Night."

The passing of the light started up front. I held the biggest chunk of my shattered candle that I could grasp. The lady next to me scowled as she passed the light of Christ to my broken candle. I lit my son's, he lit his sister's. And then my wife held up her candle to take the light from my daughter. Our eyes went wide in wonder. A perfect circle. My wife had done the impossible. She had patiently bent her candle into a perfect circle.

But then we all know it is the patience and tenderness of a mother that is often the most transformative force in the world — even if she is a Baptist.

*   *   *

TRADITIONS and customs help us know who we are. To varying degrees they shape who we are. You need to share your traditions with your kids. Part of sharing traditions is participating in activities your parents participated in with you. Go to church, fly kites, or join the Scouts. Another way to pass on traditions is through sharing stories. Tell your kids about your own childhood. Tell them where you grew up, what your parents — their grandparents — were like way back then.

My dad was a kid during World War II. He very much wanted a bicycle. During WWII there was very little spare metal. Many bicycles had been melted down to make military equipment. Dad was persistent. I imagine at times he was that kid throwing a fit in the aisle, and other times he was just diligent, bringing up the bike over and over again. He kept at it. Finally, he got the bike. He said it was so heavy he had to pedal to go down hill, but he was happy to have it.

This story taught me a lot.

It taught me what life was like when my dad

was a kid. It taught me that if you are persistent and patient you can get what you want. It taught me that you need to appreciate what you have, especially if someone made a great effort to provide it. It taught me that even though my grandparents weren't rich, they still did what they could for their children. It is nice to know that you come from a long line of good people.

If you, as an adult, didn't come from a long line of nice people, that's okay. Not every good parent had good parents to learn from. Don't let your parents' actions toward you dictate your actions toward your children. If you want to teach your children good traditions, try and remember things from your past when people did good things for you. Share those stories with your little ones.

Passing on traditions connects you and your children forward and backward—Our people have always done this and because I am teaching you, you will teach your children, so we always will do this. Be it church, or hunting, or row-boating, or banjo-picking, there is something to pass on. If not, make something up. Like bending candles.

Traditions and customs help teach a child that they are part of something bigger than themselves. When I was a kid Ronald Reagan came to town. My mom took me to see him. He was six blocks away and I just saw the top of his head, but I had seen the president. It helped me know who I was. Bruce Springsteen has a great line in the song "Long Walk Home" that has a father saying to his child, "Son, you're lucky in this town. It's a beautiful place to be born. It just wraps its arms around you. No one crowds you, nobody goes it alone. See that flag flying over the courthouse? It means certain things are set in stone. Who we are, what we'll do and what we won't." (There, I just worked Reagan and Springsteen into the same paragraph. What's that tell you about me?) I share that lyric with my children because it is true. I like my home town. It is a place where people will let you be who you are, but pick you up if you fall. And, like that flag in the song, our traditions set up our moral boundaries.

Adults

Let your kids know, and know often, what traditions are important to you. You can do this orally by telling stories, physically by being active in sports, passively by hanging your Eagle Scout badge on the wall or putting your Menorah on the shelf. Let the kids see where they come from. They may not always embrace these ideals, but they'll have a foundation on which to stand. One of the best ways to facilitate all of this is to eat meals together. Try with all your power to eat at least one meal a day with the whole clan. This gives time for conversation.

Kids

It is easy to find out about the traditions and history of your family. Ask your parents lots of questions. (Parents, don't worry, these are question you will know the answer to.) Ask your parents their funniest memory from childhood. Ask them the saddest moment from their life. Ask your parents what things we have now that they didn't have when they were kids. Ask them their favorite movie, grandma's job, the price of things when they were young… These thousand questions will teach you loads about your folks. Stories are the collected histories of everybody and one story always leads to another.

Besides eating together, I think that two of the best avenues for building connections and maintaining relationships with my kids are movies and Lego. I have been blessed with two children, one of each gender, who both love Legos and movies. They came of age during what we shall call the "Lesser Star Wars Era" in which the prequels were released. I came of age during the "Great Star Wars Era" in which the first three, and far superior, *Star Wars* movies were released. We have had a great time watching these movies together and have spent hours comparing and contrasting. (They are finally coming around to my point of view.) The Indiana Jones movies are great for this inter-generational

funfest as well. Imagine our delight when we
learned new Indy movies are on the way.

As for Lego, Lego is something you can't do wrong.
Lego is imagination in your hands. You can sit and
build whole worlds and never make a mistake
or get mad. It is a nice quiet activity where you
can have hours of conversation and accomplish
something at the same time.

It really doesn't matter what traditions you have, or
wish you had. You can always start a tradition today.

CHAPTER 5

About Eating and Mealtime

SPAM Contest

MY son is not a picky eater, so long as cereal, chicken, ice cream, and certain kinds of chips are available. He does not like surprises, unknown foods, or slimy things.

My son will enter any contest, any time, no questions asked and this is what led him to enter a SPAM eating contest even though SPAM has all the culinary qualities he hates most.

I was telling stories at Snowshoe Ski Resort as part of a spring festival. We were walking along when we heard an announcement stating that the SPAM eating contest would start in a few minutes.

"Did he say 'contest'?" my son asked.

"He said 'SPAM eating contest,'" I corrected.

"What's SPAM?"

"Spiced ham," I said.

"Canned meat," my wife said.

"Pap eats it," my daughter added. "It is sort of pinkish and covered in some sort of slime. I think it's gross." My daughter will eat most anything. She has always been an adventurous eater—she tried a raw oyster when she was four or five, and she loves alligator. She gladly eats broccoli and would rather have fruit for dessert than cookies (excepting yellow snowmen, of course.) She loves ham. For her to state that a ham product was gross was a pretty momentous statement.

"The slimy stuff is congealed fat," I added.

My son shrugged all of this information off and headed toward the table where the SPAM eating contest was going to be held. He walked up to a person who seemed to be an official and asked, "May I enter the contest?"

She looked down at my son. He was about seven

47

at the time. Everyone else surrounding the table where the contest would play out was a full grown adult. Some of the people were overgrown adults — people you would not be surprised to learn were SPAM-consuming connoisseurs. The SPAM official winked and said, "Sure."

"What's the prize?" my son asked.

The official held up a small trophy. From the look on my son's face you would have thought that she had just offered a Nobel medal as the prize for this particular pork eating showdown.

My son rubbed his hands together and took his place at the table.

The rules were pretty simple. The first person to slurp up all their SPAM, congealed fat and all, won the contest.

Several SPAM helpers walked around the table distributing cans of SPAM. The crack of the opening cans and the sucking sound of processed meat being shaken from cans filled the air.

"Where are the forks?" my son asked.

"No forks. You have to put your hands behind your back and use nothing but your face," someone explained.

"Go!" came the command.

My son, small as he was, bent to the task with zeal and vigor. Halfway through the contest he paused to gag, but fought it down and kept eating. SPAM flew through the air as the careless masticators gnashed away at the SPAM on the paper plates before them.

The sound of the slurping contestants was only slightly less disgusting then the smell of a dozen lumps of SPAM disappearing under the hot sun.

It didn't take long. One contestant licked his plate clean and was declared the winner. My son finished a close second. There was quick conversation and my son was named the winner of the seventeen and under division. He shook hands with the other contestants. He did not get a trophy, but he walked away with the heady sense of having eaten to the best of his abilities. He gave a 110%. He played every down. He had the heart (and stomach) of a champion. All of those sports clichés apply.

I was just glad that he didn't 'leave it all on the field.'

*   *   *

WE eat every day. It is a regular part of our lives. It is not always the least stressful time in our day, but we do it anyway.

Generally the day goes like this: I sleep later than everyone else so Mom and the kids eat breakfast together and I come in later. Lunch is generally a scatter-shot sort of affair involving leftovers, chicken strips, or fish sticks. My wife home schools the kids so we all eat lunch together in a fairly non-formal manner. Supper is the most formal meal of our day. We don't dress up, but the rules are a little tighter.

At breakfast we all read the paper. At lunch there are often school books on the table, or Calvin and Hobbes books, Far Side collections, and what not. Toys are allowed on the lunch table.

For supper my wife usually prepares a real meal— as opposed to something that comes straight out of the freezer and into the oven. She is not the only one who cooks. I also cook supper… on occasion. I cook maybe three or four meals a month and generally leave out at least one key ingredient.

At the supper table there are no books and no toys. We make a point of eating supper as a family and thus limit the distractions. Normally we don't answer the phone during the meal and there are no cell phones or texty things permitted at the table. It is at supper that we practice things like manners, polite ways to ask for things, how to use silverware (though it is actually tableware), and what to say if and when you accidently (or not) make a rude noise.

We start the meal with a prayer, and the kids can't leave the table until they have eaten their food and asked to be excused. After that, we do the dishes. The rule is, whoever cooks doesn't have to do the dishes. The kids and I share the task of doing the dishes and cleaning up the kitchen, but I am slowly allowing them to take on more and more of those responsibilities. My son was seven or eight when we started this; my daughter was four or five. They grumbled at first, but we explained that they needed to contribute to the household workload.

One of the issues that crops up the most around eating is that your kids won't eat or won't eat what you want them to eat. This drives me crazy and we have more or less worked through that particular frustrating phase of parenting, but it wasn't easy.

One strategy we employed early on was being careful about the portions we gave our kids. You can't put a ton of food on your child's plate and then insist that they eat it all. We put the amount of food on the plate that we want our kids to eat. If they want seconds, that's great.

I don't like English peas. Bleck. Gag. I'd rather eat congealed SPAM fat. Peas are gross and squishy.

Nobody is going to make me eat them. I try and keep this in mind when we are eating things the kids just don't like. I also don't like cooked carrots and sweet potatoes, just so you know. Or cream cheese. Or cottage cheese. Not fond of cooked spinach either. No thanks on the candied beets. Wonder where my son gets it?

My daughter, as I stated earlier, eats anything. Brussels sprouts, asparagus, collard greens? Bring it on. She is pretty easy to deal with at the table.

What we finally did with my son, as far as fruits and veggies go, is we found several fruits and vegetables that he likes, and we have those often. Our goal is to feed him a nutritious meal. If that means we eat green beans, corn, and broccoli in a regular rotation, well, that staves off trying to make him eat something he refuses to ingest. You may call it capitulation, but we call it compromise. He also loves grapes. The boy will eat a bushel of grapes. I'd rather serve him grapes and the rest of us salad if that is what it takes to get him to eat fruits and veggies.

Adults

Half of parenting is deciding your priorities. Folks tell parents all the time to "choose your battles." I'm no different. Let's face it, there are going to be plenty of things to fight about over the next eighteen years. Do you really want a throwdown about cooked carrots? A good idea my wife came up with was to require the kids to take a "No, thank-you" bite. This means that if they are presented with a dish they think they do not like, they are required to have at least a taste before saying "No, thank you." Who knows, they might like it… and you get the satisfaction of establishing a rule that gets you at least part of what you want.

Kids

Don't like what is being cooked? Cook it yourself. Ask your parents if you and your sibs can be in charge of cooking the meal every so often. Tell them they can help, but that you get to be in charge of the menu. If you are looking for revenge, find out what your parents don't like and cook that! Then make them eat their "No, thank-you" bites! Hahahaha.

About once a month we have a pizza night. It makes a mess, but by now you know I don't mind that too much. You can buy pizza dough, or make it pretty easily. There is this thing called the Internet on your computer. It will tell you how to make pizza dough. We mix up the dough and then each person gets to make their own pizza. The kids like to make theirs in various shapes and forms. Ghosts, Egyptian gods, super heroes, or whatever. Also, each person gets to apply their own sauce, cheese, veggies, and meat. This is something we do for fun—remember the rules for having fun? Don't get testy if the pizzas your kids create don't fit your image of pizza.

It takes about an hour to fix the whole meal, including the cooking, and everybody gets what they want for supper that night.

Another way we make eating fun is to have Caveman Night. On Caveman Night you come to supper in play clothes and eat with your fingers. You can grunt and tear and eat with your hands. There are no (or few) manners on Caveman Night and it is a nice break from the otherwise structured suppers we tend to have. Caveman Night works best with foods like chicken or pork chops which can easily be picked up with the hands.

Cavemen, despite what you have heard, still have to clean up after the meal and do the dishes.

CHAPTER 6

About Patience

(And believe me, I'm no expert!)

Fi-shhhhhh-ing

FISHING. Such a soothing word. So much of the inflection is put on the syllable "shing." It is almost as if people are trying to calm you down, put you to sleep, when they say the word. "Would you like to go 'fi-shhhh-ing?'" Ahh.

So, it seemed like a good idea. I asked my kids, "Do you want to go fishing?"

We were on the muddy bank of the Sunflower River in Yazoo County, Mississippi. It wasn't more than 110°. The river bank was coated in a dried layer of gumbo mud that cracked like glass when we walked across it. The dried shards where deadly sharp and chopped away at our ankles. Once the dried crust on the surface of the mud shattered, a soupy, super dense mud layer was revealed. Mud so dense it not only sucked off your shoes, but picked your pocket and read your mind as well.

The kids, of course, thought this was funny. They skipped back and forth across the mud like insects playing a dangerous game in a field of Venus Fly Traps. "Go back and get your shoes," I said as calmly as possible.

I was carrying three fishing poles, three canteens, one tackle box, one carton of fermented chicken livers, three bottles of bug spray, a box of matches, a hatchet, a cooler, and three empty five-gallon buckets. I was very slowly pushing forward through waist-deep mud, trying to stay calm.

My mantra goes like this: "You are normal. Every parent has considered selling their children to roving Gypsies. Come on Gypsies, rove on by."

Once we finally arrive at the fishing spot I expect things to go exactly as I plan. We'll set the buckets on the ground, bottoms up so we can sit on them. I'll hand out the fishing poles, spray on the bug spray, and pass around the bait. Everybody will bait up, cast, sit patiently and quietly until a fish strikes, and then we will reel them in, rejoice, and start the process again. Nice and relaxing.

I hand a bucket to my daughter. I turn to hand a bucket to my son. He has broken through the crust of the mud and is headed toward the river in an all-out slide. Moving quickly, but being careful not to begin sliding myself, I reach to rescue my son. He's waist deep in the water by the time I get a hand on his belt and drag him back to dry land. I sit him on his bucket in time to see that my daughter has made her way to the slick path my son has gouged in the mud. She is now sliding toward the river. She is shouting, "Wheeee!"

I manage to nab her before she gets wet, but only because in my haste I bust the crust and slide into the river ahead of her. I climb out of the water, smile serenely, and say, "Okay, kids, it is now time to fish." My son swats at a mosquito.

You might imagine that the mosquitoes on a central Mississippi river bank in the middle of July would be fierce. You would be wrong. They are beyond fierce. They are more inimical than an opposition congress. They are blood thirstier than any Super Pac. They suck you dry and leave you feeling icky and itchy. If your feet are stuck in the mud when the mosquitoes attack, there is a chance your legs will be left in the mud while your head and torso are carried away. And, whereas I might occasionally harbor the idea of selling my children to roving Gypsies, I would feel bad if the kids were carried off by mosquitoes. The poor mosquitoes just wouldn't know what to do with them.

I break out the Deet-free, steroid-free, MSG-free, mercury-free, fragrance-free, environmentally friendly, SPF 50, nontoxic bug spray (main ingredient: bug attractant), and douse the kids.

"Sit on your buckets," I say gently. Lovingly. "Sit on your buckets my little sweethearts and let us prepare to fish." There is a smile on my face.

I am not shouting, "Doggone it, children! We came out here to fish! Now quit messing around, get out of the mud, sit on your bucket, pick up your fishing pole, and fish!" No, no. I am not saying that. Or at least no one but the children can hear me saying that. Well, no one but the children and God. No one but the children, God, and anyone within about eight square miles of the river bank. Sound carries in the Mississippi Delta.

"Patience," I'm whispering to myself. "Just a little patience." I start to whistle the tune. I'm now taking parental advice from Axel Rose of Guns 'n Roses. How can this go poorly?

I take a deep breath and say, "Okay guys, let's get to the fishing. Bait up!"

I find that the best catfish bait in the world is chicken liver sealed in a plastic carton and left in the Mississippi sun for at least three days. The aroma is unforgettable; the texture sublimely slippery (like SPAM). The kids won't touch it. They are making faces like it is gross. I can't understand why they are so appalled by the inside of a chicken. This is fi-shhhhh-ing!

By the time I have my son's hook baited, my daughter has managed to flip her five gallon bucket over and sit on the open end. The result is that she has fallen into the bucket bottom first. Only her head, arms and legs are visible. She thinks it is hilarious. My son thinks it is hilarious. He's bigger than she is, so when he goes into the bucket he is twice as stuck as my daughter. They are laughing hysterically. I'm wondering how far they would float. Maybe some exiled group down the river needs a couple of Moseses.

Deep breath.

I extract the kids from the buckets. A swarm of mosquitoes has built a condo in my ear. A team of horseflies has decided my shoulder blade is delicious.

I bait the kids' hooks and explain again how to cast. We have Zebco reels, so they just have to push the button and swing the rod over their shoulders. My son does a pretty good job. My daughter's rod comes forward and the bait jettisons out over the river. The hook, however, is still at the end of her rod. She didn't push the button.

I cast and catch a catfish. I haul it in. It stings my hand in several places. The kids are amazed. Suddenly, they want to fish. But I still have to bait the hooks.

*   *   *

HAVE you ever found yourself trying to accomplish something with your children, teach them something, and all the while they are focused on everything else in the world? I don't know how many times I've said something which is equivalent to, "Quit enjoying that! That isn't the fun we came to have!"

Trying to teach your kids a skill or interest them in the nuances of a hobby can be difficult. You want them to enjoy the activity because the activity is important or fun to you. However, chances are, you weren't born with the skills to master the task. You had to learn. Think back, did the person who taught you the skill get frustrated and yell because you weren't focusing, or did that person let you enjoy the experience and teach you at the same time?

I'm not good at baseball. I didn't really enjoy baseball as a child because I was scared of the ball. I had a coach who got so upset about my fear that he turned me around, yelled, "Doggone it, the ball doesn't hurt that bad," and then he threw the ball at my back. Guess what? It hurt as bad as I had imagined and I never played much baseball after that.

Part of patience is perseverance. You have to remind yourself what the goal is. What are you trying to accomplish with your kids? Are trying to turn them into instant anglers, or are you trying to teach them that fishing is fun (unless you are the fish), and spending time in nature is worthwhile? Look to the goal. If my kids remember that fishing is fun because you get to sit in buckets and slide in the mud, at least they remember that fishing is fun.

I fully admit that I am not the most patient person in the world. Not even close. I want things to go the way I want them to go, and I want them to go that way now. But I do try.

Adults

Remember, you learned from someone. Your kids probably aren't going to be experts right from the start. Ask yourself, "Why do I want my child to have this skill? Am I teaching my child to catch a ball because if he doesn't learn, fire will rain from the sky, or am I teaching my child to catch a ball so he will enjoy it?"

Also, try to remember that just because you are interested in something, that doesn't mean your kids will be or that they have to enjoy it as well. Maybe it is an activity that they need to wait a few years to learn. Maybe it is something they just don't want to know. I'm not suggesting that you shouldn't teach your kids things they don't want to know. You have to teach them to write whether they want to learn or not. Table manners, in my book, are a must. These things, however, aren't learned in one sitting. Persevere. Try not to let one act at the table ruin the whole meal.

Bike riding is a classic example of something you want to be fun but starts out very frustrating. You want your child to learn to ride a bike so you gear them up with a helmet and a bike and you run behind them with one hand on the bike seat and when you let they go they scream and fall and don't want to try again. That's frustrating and you say, "Maddy, if you would just try harder you could get it. Don't be scared; just do it."

Your child probably is trying hard. And when you

are scared, having someone tell you, "Don't be scared," doesn't really help. Look at it from their point of view: If they crash it is going to hurt them, not you. Keep your cool. Try again. Try again. Smile.

Kids

There isn't much you can do here. You get the parents you get. Some adults are more patient than others. All I can tell you is that your parents aren't trying to teach you things just so that they can get frustrated and yell. If they are trying to get you to learn something, they probably think it is important. Just try your hardest, don't be scared, and tell your folks to stay cool.

CHAPTER 7

About Confidence

or

Winning and Losing

Pine Wood Derby

EACH year during Cub Scouts we had the Pine
Wood Derby. For the Pine Wood Derby each Cub
Scout got an officially sanctioned block of pine
that was about seven inches long, an inch tall, and
maybe two inches wide. The cars had no motors
but were powered by gravity alone and were thus
raced down an inclined track. The block of wood
came with four aluminum nails that were called
axles and four plastic wheels. The theory behind
the Derby was that each boy would take his block
of wood, a pocket knife, a saw, maybe a file, some
sandpaper, some paint, and create a five-ounce
race car which would then be used in competition
against cars made by other boys. Adults were

supposed to be on hand to aid the boys in the creation of their cars, but the adults were not supposed to actually build the cars.

Yeah. Right.

Each January beginning when I was seven, and ending when I was ten, I would go to my den meeting and receive my car kit. My eyes would glaze over. I would look at that block of wood and the ideas for cars would speed through my brain. I could make an Indy car. Or a wedge. Or a stock car. Or something that looked like a 1950s hot rod. Oh the plans I made as I stared at that rectangular hunk of pine! I would contemplate just how I was going to saw it, just where I was going to place the wheels, exactly how I was going to paint it, what decals I was going to stick on it. I'd sit at the den meeting and draw sketches of beautiful cars with little lines coming off the back to depict the great speed of my car as it blazed by the other cars. In my visions and sketches, all the other boys' cars looked like rectangles of pine. Each year I received that hunk of pine and, like Michelangelo, I could see the speedy David locked in the wood.

And then I would go home and give the hunk of wood to my dad. His eyes would glaze over. He would look at that block of wood and the ideas for cars would speed through his brain. He could

make an Indy car. Or a wedge. Or a stock car. Or
something that looked like a 1950s hot rod. Oh
the plans he made as he stared at that hunk of
rectangular pine! He would contemplate just how
he was going to saw it, just where he was going to
place the wheels, exactly how he was going to paint
it, what decals he was going to stick on it. He'd sit
at his desk and draw sketches of beautiful cars with
little lines coming off the back to depict the great
speed of his car as it blazed by the other cars. In his
visions and sketches, all the other dads' cars looked
like sloppy rectangles of pine. Each year he would
receive that hunk of pine and, like Michelangelo, he
could see the speedy David locked in the wood.

And I wouldn't touch that hunk of pine again until
two days before the race, when I was allowed to
spray a clear coating of sealant on the paint job.

I had two older brothers who had also been Cub
Scouts, so before I came along my dad had "helped"
build six Derby cars. And he'd never had a winner.
I had no younger brothers, so I was his last chance
to get it right. I'd sit in the workshop there in the
basement of that house on Weberwood Drive and
watch him as he measured, clamped, jig-sawed,
power sanded, drilled, graphited, smoothed, carved,
and crafted "my" cars. Sometimes he let me sand the
car—but only on the back or the bottom. That way
no one could say that he'd done all the work.

My mom would call down the steps to say, "John, *he's* supposed to be building it."

My dad would call up, "He is. He is. He's sanding it right now." Then dad would fire up the radial arm saw—which I was never, under any circumstances, allowed to touch even until this very day—and make some aerodynamically necessary improvements.

It was great fun. I loved building my Pine Wood Derby cars. One thing I got from the process was a lifelong appreciation of watching somebody else do all the work.

In all fairness, Dad did let me help some. For example, each car was supposed to weigh five ounces. To make the weight, Dad would drill holes in the bottom of the car and then fill the holes with lead. To fill the holes with lead, you had to melt the lead and pour it in. We accomplished this feat by melting fishing weights in a tin can with a propane torch. Dad let me hold the torch to melt the weights. That was cool. Watching those dull grey weights turn into bright silver liquid taught me a lot about melting points, physical and chemical changes, and even a little about the interaction of the elements on the Periodic chart. Naturally, the lead fumes made sure I never retained that information, but I sure learned it once.

Now, in the twenty-first century, we know better than to melt lead like that. It is extremely dangerous and very unhealthy. Don't do it. But, see if your dad, or uncle, or grandfather remembers doing it.

Anyway, Dad worked hard on those cars. And year after year our cars failed to take home the Gold.

My final race came when I was ten years old. It was my last year of eligibility. This was Dad's last chance. It was also Mr. Moriaty's last chance—or rather, it was Mike Moriaty's last chance. Mike and I sat watching my dad and Mr. Moriaty putting the finishing touches on "our" cars. It was about 10:30, the night before the race. And then the phone rang.

I only heard Dad's end of the conversation. It went something like, "What? Oh, hello, Christian." Christian was a kid in our Den. I don't think his mother was around anymore, and his father had Black Lung, or some other debilitating respiratory disease. "You what?" Dad asked. "Well, why didn't you call earlier? Like last week? Um-hum. Okay. Sit tight. I'll be right there."

Dad hung up and looked at Mr. Moriaty. "Christian needs a car. He didn't think about calling until just now. I'm gonna go get him."

"It's too late," Mr. Moriaty said.

"Well," Dad said, "we'll have to do something for the kid."

Dad got in the car and drove over to pick Christian and his hunk of pine up. Christian sat beside me and Mike while Dad and Mr. Moriaty did what they could. They'd spent days making my car, and Mike's. They now had mere hours to build Christian's. My dad rounded the edges of the car with his pocket knife, gave it a once over with the electric sander, and then he let Christian put a coat of paint on the hunk of wood. Dad slapped the wheels on without even adjusting or balancing them.

"At least," he said to Christian, "you'll be able to compete."

"Thanks," Christian said.

Well, you guessed it. Dad had built his winner. Christian's hastily carved, barely sanded, poorly painted car won the whole competition. Beat every other car that entered. My car didn't even place. Mike Moriaty's car didn't place. But Dad had his winner.

Now, you might think the moral of this story is—"If you leave things to the last minute, you'll probably win the whole race." But that is not the moral to this tale. Nor is the moral, "The less you do, the better you'll do." Nope. In fact, it's not even moral time because that isn't even the end of the story.

You see, I grew up. I had a son. And he joined the Cub Scouts. One night in January they handed out those hunks of pine, with the four aluminum nails for axles, and the four plastic wheels. I looked at my son as he stared at that piece of wood, dreaming of how his car would look, how he would cut it, carve it, sand it, and paint it. I could see the dreams of an Indy car in his eyes. Of a stock car. Of a hotrod.

And I remembered how much, when I was a kid, I'd wanted to make my own Pine Wood Derby car.

I said to my son, "Let me help you with that." And I cut and I sawed and I sanded and I chiseled and I painted and I balanced and graphited the wheels— and you know what? We won second place.

I got home from the race and called my dad. I told him we'd won second place and then I said, "See. You should have let me build my own cars. You might 'a won."

So, the moral of this story is this: Kids—build your own cars. Do your own thing. Wrestle that block of wood from your dad's hand and do it yourself. But, don't be selfish. He really wants to help. Maybe let him sand the bottom and the back.

And, if he wants, let him put the decals on. He's probably pretty good at that.

*　　　*　　　*

WE all want our children to succeed. We want them to gain the feelings of accomplishment and confidence that come with a job well done. What we forget is that a job well done doesn't necessarily mean a check in the win column. The idea that your child is always going to finish first in all of his or her endeavors is unrealistic, and you know it. If we teach our kids that the only successful outcome is total victory than we are not going to raise confident children, but rather nervous little neurotics who worry constantly that they won't live up to the standards we have set for them. Let us pledge to not raise nervous little neurotics.

I tell my kids fairly often, "No matter how fast, smart, funny, or good you are, someone is going to come along who is faster, smarter, funnier, or better." I do not say this to belittle my children, but to prepare and inspire them. If they have a talent in a field in which they want to succeed, I want them to strive to be the best, and in order to strive to better themselves they need to not become complacent. If you believe you are the best, why try to get better?

71

I also tell my children, "Do your best." And when they encounter a loss or a disappointment I ask them, "Did you do your best?" If the answer is "Yes," then we all know that the world is not over, we can take pride in our actions, and perhaps we need to train or work a little harder to prepare for next time.

I imagine it stings to win the Silver medal at the Olympics. I imagine that for about a week you walk around thinking, "Oh man, 0.04 seconds faster and I would have won." I also imagine that after about a week your mood swings and you start smiling and thinking, "Well, by golly, I got the Silver medal at the Olympics." There is, in most of us, a competitive edge, but success does not always mean finishing first.

Conversely, continually participating in activities in which there is no winner doesn't teach our children anything. When kids play T-ball or football or soccer and the rules state "There is no winner. Everyone who plays is a winner!" I cringe. What does that teach anybody? No matter if your kids go into art, business, non-profit community work, or competitive fishing, there is always going to be competition. You are always going to be competing against some person or some organization for resources. Kids need to learn that they must to do their best in all their activities if they are going to have a viable chance at taking on the world. If you aren't playing to win, what's the incentive to get better?

I have not yet been to a game where "we don't keep score" is the rule when my kids have not come off the field and told me how many points or runs were scored, and which team won or lost. Your kids are keeping score.

I grew up a very poor athlete, a bad speller, and not very good at much else. I was often picked last when teams were chosen, put on losing teams, and out first in games of elimination. Be it dodge ball or spelling bees, getting out first stings. Did it make me feel bad? Yes. Did it crush me? No. It made me do two things. It made me strive to be better, and it made me look for activities in which I had talent. I'll never be a professional ball player, but I am proud to say that at the time of this writing I hold the record for the one mile run at our local YMCA, and not just in my age division.

My parents encouraged me to play sports and participate in activities. Win or lose, they rubbed my head on the way off the field. No hard feelings. (Honestly, I don't think it took long for them realize that there wasn't much need to bet on my getting an athletic scholarship, so there was no sense being bent out of shape about my inabilities.)

For as long as I can remember I wanted to be a writer. My parents encouraged that. I have a box, a big box, on my book shelf full, and I mean full, of rejection letters from publishers regarding my work. If I had been brought up believing that winning is the only way to succeed I would not have kept on writing. The arts, and many other fields, are conquered not by strings of victories, but continual perseverance after loss and rejection.

You have got to let kids do things themselves. Let them paint without telling them what colors to use. Who cares if their chicken looks like a surrealistic lizard? Again, kids see the world differently than adults. They quantify and qualify things differently. It is their way of exploring the world. Imagination is not just a function of the brain, but a process through which we explore the world. A child painting an upside down house is asking the question "What if?" And they are creating the answer. Remember that yellow snowmen cookies are just as delicious as white ones.

Find ways to do things like science projects and pinewood derby cars that allow both of you to take an active part.

When it came time for my son to make Pine Wood Derby cars I started by asking him, "What do you want your car to look like?" The two most

memorable answers were, "A submarine," and
"A chariot." My daughter, who also made a car,
asked for a shoe. Good gracious. I'm a writer and
a storyteller. Not a sculptor. I used what limited
skills I had to rough out the various shapes. The
kids then took over with the carving, the sanding
and the painting. (Okay, full disclosure, I did a lot
of sanding while they were asleep, and my wife
touched up the paint jobs.) I got on the internet and
researched high tech Pine Wood Derby technology,
but eventually reminded myself that one of the
reasons we build these cars is to give the kids the
opportunity to learn how to use tools like saws,
files, sandpaper, and paint brushes (so they can
build their kids' cars).

It is a learning experience, not the Daytona 500.

We resolved early on that we weren't going to
have the prettiest cars, and maybe not even the
fastest cars, but we were going to enjoy the time
spent building them. We also let the kids paint
the bottoms of the cars in any crazy fashion they
desired.

One year we won. Not the race, but most creative car.

CHAPTER 8

About Reading and Language Arts

Reading from the Start

I was the last of five kids. When you are the last of
five kids everyone assumes everyone else taught
you what you need to know. If you manage to learn
anything at it all it is usually by sheer accident. I
was nine before I realized nobody in my family was
named Who's-gonna. As in, "Who is gonna change
the baby?" or "Who is gonna feed the baby?" I was
eleven before I knew the difference between my
elbow and my shoulder.

I know my parents read to me. I remember
various episodes when Mom or Dad read books
to me. I remember very clearly my dad reading
The Grinch Who Stole Christmas every Christmas.

I also remember my dad telling me stories such as Goldilocks and the Seven Bears, or Sleeping Beauty and the Three Billy Goats Gruff. I don't know why he told me these mixed-up versions of the fairy tales. They were certainly funnier the way he told them, but I don't know if he told skewed versions because after having told the stories to four other children, he was just bored with the normal versions, or because he just didn't know the real stories. At any rate, they were entertaining stories and certainly influenced my career. What I don't remember is being read to a lot. Maybe I was. Maybe it is one of those things that happened that I just don't recall. I mean, I don't recall many specific instances of eating as a child either, but I'm pretty sure I ate regularly.

I want my kids to remember me reading to them.

My wife and/or I have read to our children almost every night of their lives. My eldest recently arrived at the time in his life when he would rather read to himself. That was a bittersweet moment. I was glad we had instilled a love of reading but sorry to let those nightly moments go. My youngest still likes me to read to her, but the writing, so to speak, is on the wall. She is getting to where she reads quite well herself and most nights now she reads to me.

I'm an avid reader with wide and sometimes eclectic

tastes, but I didn't really start to read recreationally until I was probably a sophomore in college. I have never been tested, but it would not surprise me to learn that I have at least a mild reading disability. I often see letters in a different order than other folks. I read very slowly. My wife, also an avid reader, can read an encyclopedia in the time it takes me to read Fox in Sox. We want our kids to be avid readers, so we read to them.

I am not a scientist or a pediatrician, but I've read the same studies you have, and reading to your kids helps them immensely when it comes to their speech, vocabulary, comprehension, reading ability, and language arts in general.

When my son was just a few months old I started working on his vocabulary. I would lie in the bed and hold him over me airplane style—well, I guess he wasn't that young, his neck must have been working by this point—and then I would lower him to my face and say a word such as, "Occupy," then lift him again. Then I would lower him and say something such as, "Signify," then "Rectify," and so on. Once he rewarded me for this game by throwing up into my mouth. I know he had no idea what I was talking about, but I firmly believe it helped him develop the vocabulary he has now. And I learned yet another lesson in keeping my mouth closed when there is any unobstructed line between my face and any baby orifice.

My son started reading when he was about three. This is despite the fact that I was secretly teaching him the alphabet in the wrong order. He was doing pretty well until my wife discovered my secret. She didn't think it was nearly as funny as I did. He reads the comics in the paper every day. His favorite is Garfield. At one point, our paper decided to cut Garfield from the paper. My son, then five or six years old, was incensed. So, I showed him how to write a letter to the editor. The paper relented and Garfield came back. Now, not only does he read, but he also understands social activism.

My daughter took a bit longer to learn to read, but she has always enjoyed being read to. And she loves books. One of the things she loves most about books is making books. Ever since she could wield a pen she has been illustrating books. Before she could write she would create elaborate books of drawings and then she would dictate the words and I would write them on the pages for her. After that, she would ask me to make copies, staple them together, and she would go door to door selling them. It is easy to sell books when you go door to door and you are cute.

Another way we have introduced our children to reading and language is by letting them listen to books on tape at night. I guess a less antiquated way to say that is, we let our kids listen to recorded books. They read before they go to bed and then they listen to books being read as they fall asleep. I don't know how many books they have listened to, but it is bunches. They often listen to books they have already read. I know that the Magic Tree House series has been read and heard in our house several times over.

A benefit of my job (I'm a professional storyteller who tours the country) is that my kids get to listen to stories all the time, and from the best storytellers in the country. For as long as my kids have been alive they have been going to several storytelling festivals a year. Hearing stories, like reading, opens the mind to creative ways of thinking. Listening to a story, like reading, is good work for the brain. Unlike watching TV or a movie, when you simply listen to a story, or read a book, your mind has to do a lot more work. The director of a motion picture has a very clear idea of how she wants you to see the story, and she is not going to put anything on the screen that she does not want you to see. You don't have to imagine much to watch a movie, and you aren't offered much opportunity to mentally improvise. When you listen to a story your brain has to do a lot more work. Listening to a story gives your child's mind the chance to hear the words and then process the words in any manner they see fit. Listening engages the mind and opens the brain to a mental free-for-all. Your child's brain, when listening to a story, or listening to you read, is working on several levels. Your child is processing the words, sorting and defining the words, figuring out how the words work together, painting the scenery, creating an image of the characters, and keeping a chronological and biographical index of the events and people in the story. That's a heck of a workout for your kid's brain, and it has to be good for them.

*   *   *

THERE is no substitute for reading. It is going to make your children smarter people. I know your days are busy and there are a hundred other things to do. I have found that bedtime is sometimes the most stressful time of the day. Your kids don't want the fun to end, and you know that once the kids are down you can finally have an hour or two to do adult stuff. So, after overseeing the process of putting on pajamas and brushing teeth and getting children into bed, adding five, ten, or thirty minutes to the process by reading to your kids may seem daunting. It is worth it though, immensely worth it.

You don't need to read for an hour. If your kids are small then their books are short. You can buzz through a couple of picture books in a matter of minutes. My daughter is eight and still loves picture books. The text and subject matter have grown more complex, but it still doesn't take very long to read a thirty-two page book that is mostly pictures. If you just can't squeeze reading into the nightly schedule then set aside one night a week to read.

We have two kids and for just one adult to read to both of them individually added a lot of time to the bedtime process. If we had more kids than that I'm not sure we could have managed to read to each kid individually every night. However, there is nothing wrong with reading to all, or several, of your kids at once. For a few years there, we would all get into one bed (you gotta rotate through the kids' beds to keep politic) and read one book my daughter would select, one from my son, and often a bit of a chapter book they were both interested in such as *Alice in Wonderland* or *Charlotte's Web*.

If all else fails, read the comics from the paper to your kids during breakfast. Or at supper if you get the evening news.

Kids

Bug your parents to read to you. Actually, if they are reading this book then there is a pretty good chance that they are already reading to you, but bug them anyway. Carry books around in your grimy little children hands and say, "Read this to me, please."

If you don't have any books in your house then get your adults to take you to the library!

Adults

The library is a wonderful place. Just about every library I have ever been to has a children's section, and while most librarians are great proponents of treating books with respect, they also understand that grubby-handed little children are necessarily going to inflict a little distress into the lives of books. Take your kids to the library and give them the liberty to scour the shelves for themselves. Picking books that they want to read is a fantastic personal freedom. Let your kids crawl through the stacks and select books that look good to them. Your children are going to judge books by their covers, but who cares? Let them choose some of the books they take home. Of course you want to steer some of the choices—you are the person who is going to have to read some of this stuff—but don't be a dictator.

Parenthetically, my kids both have library cards and the library is not a bad place to start teaching personal and financial responsibility. Each child can check out as many books as the library allows, but each child is also responsible for keeping track of those books and returning them on time. Any fines incurred by the kids are paid by the kids.

As you read together, kids and adults, you can ask each other questions. Ask each other how the different characters might sound. If you are reading a picture book try and pick which character is which in the pictures. When we read *Alice in Wonderland* we went through the book looking at the illustrations before we read the book. Some of the pictures really stirred our curiosity and made getting to the pages on which those illustrations were a common goal. We looked forward to finding out what was going on on those pages.

You can also take the time to discuss why the characters acted the way they did, why they made certain decisions, and what you would have done in a similar situation. I believe that one of the most useful functions of a book is that the characters encounter events and situations in their lives that we may encounter in our own. Those events might be sad, or scary, or exciting, or morally questionable. By seeing how the characters in books react, we can begin to understand how we might react in similar situations. Books can be a useful real-life situation simulator.

When my kids were learning to read for

themselves I would often get them to read portions of the books I was reading to them. This might mean alternating sentences, or pages, or paragraphs. If your child is reluctant to share the task of reading (I think both my kids were afraid that if they learned to read we would quit reading to them) you can always trick them. Tricking your kids, after all, is one the great pleasures of parenting. I would often insert silly things into the text I was reading. If the text read, "They were very, very tired," I might say, "They were very, very, very, very, very, very, very...." And I would keep saying very until one child protested. My child would say, "It doesn't say that!" And then I would ask them to prove it, at which point the child would have to read the text themselves to see if I was correct or not. Or, I would insert the absurd: "Tarzan heard the cry of the lion. He launched himself off the branch and reached for a vine. However, Tarzan hadn't been working out lately and had been eating a lot of ice cream. As a result, the vine broke and Tarzan fell twelve stories. He landed in the middle of the road and was hit by a truck."

Children, you can play this game, too. Tell your adult that you want to read, and then see what nonsense you can invent before they catch on to you.

I also encourage you to go to storytelling festivals.

Again, my job is being a storyteller so I have a vested interest in you going to festivals, but I want you to go for your own good, not just for me!

Storytelling festivals generally present several tellers from many cultural backgrounds, so not only will your children, and you, get to hear stories and tales from all over the world, but you will learn about history, religion, sociology, anthropology, and so much more. Beyond those subjects, and as I said earlier, storytelling will present opportunities for your child's mind to work and grow on many different levels at once. Listening to stories is a workout for the brain.

Storytelling is also a great way to spend time with your family. Even though you are sitting and listening in a somewhat formal audience/presenter atmosphere, storytelling is a very communal event. Storytelling by nature is a function of community.

The main thing is, both kids and adults, be it through books or stories, get your mind going. Find time to share in language arts together!

CHAPTER 9

About Faith and Prayer and Giving

Why Are We Praying for Raymond?

EVERY evening before supper, we pray. Generally we pray the Philmont Grace. The Philmont Grace is a traditional Boy Scout prayer that originated, presumably, at Philmont Scout Ranch. It goes:

> For food, for raiment
>
> For life, for opportunity
>
> For friendship and fellowship
>
> We thank thee oh Lord
>
> Amen.

"Raiment" means clothes.

This led both our children to pray "For food, for Raymond…" at some point during the prayer learning curve. "Who is Raymond?" was the logical question that followed. "And why are we praying for him?"

"He's the guy that checks us out at the grocery store," was one answer my wife gave.

"But sometimes," my daughter pointed out, "a woman checks us out at the store."

"Her name is Raymond, too," explained my wife.

Kids will believe anything.

"It means clothes," I said.

"'Raymond' means clothes?" my son asked.

"Sure, most names mean something."

Eventually they learned that "raiment" means clothes and that we were not praying for Raymond—not that we have anything against Raymond.

Our neighbors use the prayer:

God is great

God is good

So we thank him for our food.

We don't use this particular prayer because it got into my head that if you were looking at this prayer for the first time it looks like "good" and "food" would rhyme. If "good" and "food" rhymed, you would pronounce "food'" "fude" or... well, I can't figure out to spell it, but just say it out loud. Go ahead, say "food" but pronounce it so it rhymes with "good." I mentioned this to my kids and ever since, as irreverent as it may be, we can't get through that prayer without giggling. And now I wish you good luck getting through that prayer yourself.

My wife and I have a pretty simple answer to the question, "Why do we pray before supper?" That answer is, "Because we are thankful to God for providing us with all that we have. Everything we have is a gift from God and a suppertime prayer is a good way to remind ourselves of that fact."

We don't have as a good an answer to the question, "How come we don't pray at breakfast and lunch?" We are just as thankful for those meals, I assure you, but those meals are also more scattered and less formal, so we generally only pray at supper...

but it is a multi-meal prayer. We pray for supper at home and we often, but not always, pray for supper when we dine out, but the formality thing kicks in there, too. I think we are more likely to pray at a steak house then we are at a buffet or Burger King. I assure you that we are just as thankful for the food. It must have something to do with the ambience. Note to self—Pray at Burger King.

We are United Methodists. Well, no we aren't. We most often go to a United Methodist church, but we sometimes go to a Christian non-denominational church. My wife is Baptist, good old Southern Baptist from when she grew up in Mississippi. We don't go to a Baptist church. The point is, we go to church most Sundays when we are home. Because we travel a lot, we sometimes miss church. The point is, we try to go to church but we are not perfect. But then, if we were perfect we wouldn't need to go to church at all.

Funny things happen at church. One Sunday a lady in the pew in front of us passed out, cold. She wasn't overcome by the Holy Spirit or invaded by demons (those sorts of things seldom happen in Methodist churches), she was just ill. Someone shouted, "Get a glass of water!" My son, Boy Scout to the core and prepared to administer first aid to save a life, ran to get the water. He then ran back into the sanctuary and promptly threw the water from the glass on the lady. "What are you doing?" came a chorus of voices. My son, about 10 at the time, shrugged and said, "Well, that's what they do in the movies when people faint." Nobody could fault him for that. We had a chuckle, the lady recovered, and church resumed.

A week before Easter several years ago my daughter's Sunday school class walked barefoot through mud and then took turns washing each other's feet. After the class my wife asked my daughter, "What did you learn from that?"

My daughter lifted her chin and announced, "We learned humiliation." Of course, she meant humility.

So, whether it be for breakfast or supper, for clothes or for Raymond, to save our souls or others' lives, or to learn humiliation or humility, we will continue to pray and to go to church. You never know what may come of it.

*   *   *

I grew up going to church every Sunday. I don't know how you grew up. Maybe you grew up going to a ward, or a mosque, or a temple, or a shrine, or nowhere at all on Sunday morning. It may not be kosher to say, but I think when you are raising children it is important to instill faith in their lives.

I grew up a Christian and so my point of view is necessarily slanted in that direction, but in this chapter I am not trying to sway you to my faith. I'm just saying you should teach your children your faith, and this is what that looks like to me.

I didn't necessarily like church and spent a lot of the time doodling or drooling in church. I am glad my parents made me go, though. I think it is important to have faith in something bigger than yourself. I am not the sort of religious person who spends a good bit of time trying to convince others that they should repent or convert—maybe I should be—but I tend to be low key in my faith. I try to live and act like a Christian, and let my life be an example for my children and for others. I also try not to engage in religious arguments over things like which religion is best, what denomination someone needs to be, Creation vs. Evolution, the gender of God… I tell my kids that the most important thing we can do is remember that God created the universe and be thankful for the things we have. I tell them it doesn't matter to me how God created the universe. I refuse to limit God's ability to create. If God created through a big bang, or over seven days, or through evolution, or if the world sits on the back of a turtle, then that was a decision God made and God didn't ask my opinion. The important thing is that God created the universe.

The next most important thing, I tell my kids, is that God created us to help others. God wants us to be out there feeding the hungry, clothing the poor, and doing unto others what we would have them do unto us. If you have read the Bible and missed this message, then you read a different Bible than I did.

This is turning into a sermon, but I think that if we teach our children that all of our life is a gift and because of that we should be thankful and strive to serve those who are less fortunate, then we can make the world a better place. Simple, right?

One last, and possibly controversial idea, and then I'll change the subject. I have told my children that one of the things that give Christians a bad name in the world is that when we make the news it is often because we are against something. When the *Harry Potter* books first came out, Christians far and wide decried the books as evil and anti-Christian. Many Christians spent a considerable amount of time openly hating the *Harry Potter* series. They made posters and went on TV. How much good, I ask my kids, could those people have done if instead of spending all that time and energy hating *Harry Potter* they had used that time to feed the poor? I think Christians should strive to be inclusive and loving, rather than exclusive and hateful.

Adults

Tell your children what you believe in. Make the effort to go to worship once a week. Find a prayer that suits you and pray over a meal. Let your kids see you giving a dollar to a homeless guy on the street. People say, "Well he's just going to use that money to buy wine," or whatever. I like to ask those people just what they were going to do with that money. Were they going to spend it on something useful, or frivolous? Don't let your children hear you sneer that somebody should get a job, or doesn't deserve your help because they don't look or think like you. No matter what you think, you didn't get to where you are in your life by yourself. Somebody somewhere along the line had a little mercy and gave you a boost, whether you know it or not. None of us are more than one or two bad decisions away from a life of destitution.

Kids

Look out into the world and see if there is anybody you can help. Encourage your adults to help others. If your parents say things like, "We can't give that man money—he'll just buy booze," then ask your parents to carry gift cards to McDonalds or Wendy's with them. That way, when you see a panhandler you can give them a gift card that they can only use to get food.

When we go to big cities I give my kids spare
change so that they can give that money to street
performers, or hungry people, or whomever they
choose. It teaches them to love others, and that
is what God wants us to do. Go ahead, ask your
adults for a couple of quarters.

CHAPTER 10

About Individuality

The Boy Who Could Not Say a Thing

ONCE there was a boy who knew every word. He tried with all his might to use each word every day. Sometimes he imagined that he was a breath of wind. He imagined that all the words in the world were like seeds on a fluffy white dandelion. He pretended that if he did not blow the seeds off of the stem then those words would wither and die.

Sometimes he imagined he was a bee. It was his job to fly from word tree to word tree, pollinating all the words in the world.

His name was Jonah. And Jonah started talking the moment he awoke. From that point on, words fell out of his mouth like jellybeans until the moment he fell asleep.

Jonah talked for hours on end without ever really saying anything at all—except the words themselves. He had all the words organized in his head like lures in a well-kept tackle box. He could open the box and cast out any combination of words.

But you had to listen closely to Jonah because every now and then there would be a question, or a statement, lodged between the lists of words. Jonah would come down to breakfast and say things like:

> Furthermore, sunflower, stone, monkey, feather. May I have some toast, please? Shoe, run, sunshine, mile marker, fun.

It was hard for his parents to keep track of all that he said. Sometimes they got frustrated and said, "You are just talking to make noise." Or, "You are going to use all your words up before you have said anything at all." And sometimes, when they'd had it up to here (or '"hear"—ha, ha), they'd say, "Jonah, for one minute just shut your mouth!"

Jonah would try to keep his mouth closed for one minute. But he felt the words building up inside of him. It was like trying to hold back a sneeze.

Even at night he would lie in bed and talk until he drifted off to sleep. He would see his words light the dark like fireflies as he would say:

> Thank you for Grandma and Grandpa and Me-me and Pap and Kaylen and Glynn and Ashleigh and Austin and Moe and Mommy and Daddy... ZZZZZZZZZ

Jonah had a sister named Moe. Moe hardly spoke at all. She left most of the word-sowing to her brother. However, Moe liked to draw. She loved the colors and the lines and the swirls of the world. She knew words were important, but she felt it was equally important for the world to be able to express itself in pictures.

As far as Moe was concerned, it was more important, for example, to see a sunflower than to simply say 'Sunflower.' She thought, "You can say, 'I saw a sunflower.' And when you say that, people will know what you mean. But the word 'Sunflower' is always the same, whereas each sunflower in the world is different."

Moe thought that sometimes it was more important to communicate with colors than words.

She would draw for hours on end. But you had to pay attention to the pictures because sometimes there would be a statement or a question in the drawing.

She would draw things like:

Which meant, "It's a beautiful day, Daddy. Get out of bed. Drink your coffee and take me on a bike ride."

Sometimes Moe drew what Jonah said. Sometimes Jonah said what Moe drew. Sometimes Jonah said what Jonah said while Moe drew what Moe drew.

Sometimes Jonah's words fell out of the air and dropped on Moe's paper. Other times, Moe's pictures would fly off the page and turn into Jonah's words. Many times the words and pictures mingled together. They helped each other open the windows and doors. Then the words and pictures would dance and twist together out into the sky for the world to use.

One time Moe was in a joking mood and she drew:

By which she meant, "I bet if Jonah could not talk he would swell up, turn blue, and explode."

And you know what? She was right.

At the very moment Jonah saw the drawing, his father said, "Jonah, please, I'm trying to hear the news. Could you stop talking for sixty seconds?"

Jonah nodded and shut his mouth. After twenty seconds the inside of his nose started to tingle, then burn. It felt like he'd burped a soda burp in his nose. He reached up and squeezed his lips together. He needed to talk! Then he looked at Moe's drawing again and began to get worried. What if he did explode?

He hiccupped. His belly shook and a word broke loose. He wanted to let his father hear the news so he tried to swallow the word back down. It jammed in his voice box and he could not say a thing.

He could breathe, but he could not utter a sound.

Moe cleared her throat and said softly, "Something is wrong."

Their mother looked up from the magazine she was reading. For a moment she was confused. Then she said, "The boy is not talking! He's breathing, but not talking!"

Jonah was beginning to swell. A button flew off his shirt and bounced off the wall.

"What's wrong, son?"

Jonah pointed to his throat but his father did not understand. Jonah felt words crashing together in his throat, getting tangled and misspelled.

Moe held up the picture she had drawn:

The father said, "Ah, yes. I understand. 'Can't talk. Going to explode.' Quite frightening. He was trying to be quiet for sixty seconds, as I'd asked. I think the words are stuck in his throat."

"Oh my stars and gardenias!" said their mother. "What shall we do?"

Jonah was worried that all the words cluttered in his neck were being lost.

For the first time in their lives, Father and Mother said to their son, "Say something, boy!"

Jonah sneezed. The letters 'J' and 'Q' came out of his mouth. An 'H' came out of his nose. 'H' is not a pleasant letter to have come out of your nose. An 'M' came out of his ear.

Jonah began to swell like a balloon. More buttons flew off his shirt.

"This is rather distressing," said Father. "We should probably take him outside."

Then Jonah reached out and put his hand on Moe's shoulder. The jumbled words of an idea flowed silently down Jonah's arm and onto his sister's shoulder. Then the words slid down her skin and into her hand. She reached out and picked up some crayons. She stuck her tongue out of the corner of her mouth and drew hurriedly, but not hastily:

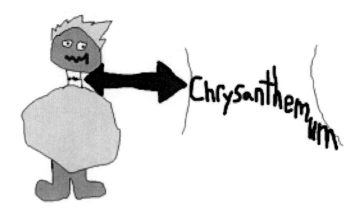

"Yes," said Mother, looking at the drawing.

"I see," said Father.

"He's got the word 'Chrysanthemum' jammed in his throat," they said together.

Father, knowing first aid because he was an Eagle Scout, whacked the boy smartly between the shoulder blades.

"Chrysan..." gurgled the boy.

His father whacked him again.

102

"… themum," choked Jonah as the word sprang free of his throat.

Jonah smiled awkwardly and put a hand on his belly.

Moe said softly, "You'd best grab hold of him."

Jonah felt the tangle of words lodged in his throat begin to sort themselves out. He was almost two minutes behind schedule. He had to let the words into the world.

Father grabbed at Jonah, knowing a torrent of words was coming. He knew words were going to burst forth from his son like burning rocket fuel.

Jonah opened his mouth and words began pouring out. First small words put themselves together and escaped the fray in his neck. They came out of his mouth like Scrabble blocks, organized themselves, and flew off toward the clouds. Then bigger words emerged, floating like streamers into the air. Then still bigger words materialized. These latter words were heavy and needed to flap their syllables to gain enough momentum to zoom into the atmosphere.

Word upon word that had been jammed behind "chrysanthemum" shot out of Jonah's mouth. Jonah would have indeed blasted off had his father not grabbed his ankle at the very last moment. For twenty-two minutes showers and flames and columns and rows and phalanxes of words rushed from Jonah's mouth.

He quoted Shakespeare. He sang hymns and carols. He

103

delivered speeches. Finally he said, "An infinite number of monkeys."

And then he turned to his sister and said, "Thank you. I was afraid we might lose a few there. Instead, I think I let an out extra dose of words today."

Moe nodded and smiled. Then she held up the picture she'd been drawing while Jonah's words were loosing themselves. It was a colorful portrait of a river. The whitewater crashed over boulders and waterfalls. Fish were leaping against the current trying to get up stream. Bears frolicked in the water, trying to catch the fish. Colorful birds sat in blooming fruit trees. Bees buzzed. Dandelion seeds filled the breeze. Fireflies sparkled on the darkening horizon.

Moe said to Jonah, "It was the most beautiful thing you ever said."

Jonah said, "I had no idea I said all those colors and swirls and twists."

Mother and Father said, "What would the world do without the two of you?"

*　　　　*　　　　*

THERE is not much to add to this.

Adults

Your kids are who they are. You brought them into this

world, they are composed of your DNA, and you need to help shape and construct their minds and ideals so that they can be productive members of society, but you don't get to say who they are. Each child has a personality and in the end our job is to help your child fit his or her personality into the world. You can't make your child be something she is not.

Does this mean if your child is an artist you shouldn't make them learn math? Of course not. The essentials are the essentials. If your kid isn't a great athlete, that's no excuse for them not being fit. You as the adult need to do some of the driving to make sure your kid is ready for the world. You, however, don't get to say who they will be or what they will do. We all have dreams and hopes for our kids, but you have to remember that they have hopes and dreams as well. Take pride in what your kids can do and like to do: don't be disappointed if they don't exceed at the things you hoped they would.

If your kids have an interest in something, be it karate, ballet, accounting, basketball, or quilting, find a way to get them instruction in that area. You may not be crazy about it, but let them explore. Besides, they may figure out they don't really want to be a world class arborist after all, but let them make that decision.

Kids

If you have an interest, follow the dream. Parents don't always believe you are really interested in something until you've brought it up 1000 times. If you like to paint but your parents won't buy you a paint set just keep doodling on the napkins until somebody takes the hint.

Your adults have a weird idea that you are little versions of themselves and that they are going to make the world right by making sure you do things the way they wish they had done things. That's a big burden for you. There are times when your parents are right. When your mother says, "No, you may not be a stock car racer when you are eight," she probably has valid safety concerns in mind. Your parents want to keep you safe. Sometimes keeping you safe means, to them, steering you away from talents and jobs that they think aren't very stable. But keep at it.

If you like to draw, draw. If you like to talk, talk. You never know where it will take you.

CHAPTER 11

Final Note

So, there you go. You're ready to go out and parent.

If only it were that simple.

I appreciate you reading my book, and I hope it helps. As I said before, I'm no expert. I'm just muddling through. I make mistakes everyday as a parent and I can have a short fuse, but I try to stay cool, teach, and have a little fun along the way. I try to remember that my goal as a parent is to raise children who will contribute to society, be nice to people, and help those in need. I also try to remember that my children will probably be parents someday and that the way I raise my kids will affect the way they raise their kids. I want to set a good example. I want my children to look back and remember me fondly, but I'll be most proud if they remember that I was a good father and that I prepared them for adulthood. I'm not trying to be my children's best friend; I'm trying to be their best dad. That means that there are times when I, or my wife, have to draw lines and receive the ire of our children for denying them something they want or want to do. There will be strife, but part of parenting is being ready to stand firm. I'm fond of the conversation that goes, "But Elmore's mom let him do it!" And then I get to say, "Well, I guess Elmore has nicer parents than you." I'm not in a competition with other parents and neither are you. That doesn't mean you can't learn from other parents, though. When you are out in public, watch other parents. See how they treat their children and make a mental note of the behaviors you want to adopt or avoid. I know I have done things or said to things to my kids that would make me cringe if I saw or heard another parent do the same to their children. Making mistakes doesn't disqualify you from being a good parent, but do strive to be better every day.

I try to find things to do with each child individually. I am an Assistant Scoutmaster for my son's troop, and I take my daughter to her piano lessons and take an active role in her daily piano practice. It doesn't look like much on paper, but when you add all the hours over the years I put into those activities with each kid, it adds up to a lot of individual, special attention paid to each child. Even if you have eleven kids, try and find something special to do with each of them. I also do things with my kids that are primarily "Dad & Kid" time. The three of us like to go to the movies together. We buy a big tub of popcorn and a huge drink, and share it through the movie. After the movie we talk about the previews and what we want to see next. And we discuss the movie itself. It's a nice way to spend the afternoon.

My wife has her things that she does with the kids without me. For example, she does most of the kids' schooling and coaches the swim team. We're not trying to exclude each other, but rather build bonds with the children that will help pull us through trouble spots. A house built on the rock, a solid foundation, and all of that.

Of course, we do things as a family as well. We take walks after supper, play disc golf, go camping, and so on. There's a whole world out there; grab the kids and go.

You had the kids—now make the time and sacrifice to raise them well.

Finally, a message for the children: Your parents are

trying. They really are. If they read this book then they are making an effort to do their best for you. You are not always going to agree with your parents, but you need to believe that they are acting in your best interest. Your folks might be rich, they might be poor, but they are doing what they can for you with what they have. Tell them thanks every now and again. Tell them you love them. Smile at them when they seem down, pat them on the back and say, "You're a good dad," or "You're a good mom." Trust me, they'll appreciate it. Oh, and make your bed, take out the trash, feed the dog, clean your room, do your homework, and the most classic advice of all—Eat every carrot and pea on your plate! Go ahead, say that last part out loud. It'll make you giggle.

About the Publisher

FAMILIUS was founded in 2012 with the intent to align the founders' love of publishing and family with the digital publishing renaissance which occurred simultaneous with the Great Recession. The founders believe that the traditional family is the basic unit of society, and that a society is only as strong as the families that create it.

Familius' mission is to help families be happy. We invite you to participate with us in strengthening your family by being part of the Familius family. Go to www.familius.com to subscribe and receive information about our books, articles, and videos.

Website: www.familius.com
Facebook: www.facebook.com/paterfamilius
Twitter: @familiustalk
Pinterest: www.pinterest.com/familius

CPSIA information can be obtained at www.ICGtesting.com
Printed in the USA
BVOW041653280213

314358BV00001B/1/P